T0055745

TCHAIKOVSKY'S
THE NUTCRACKER

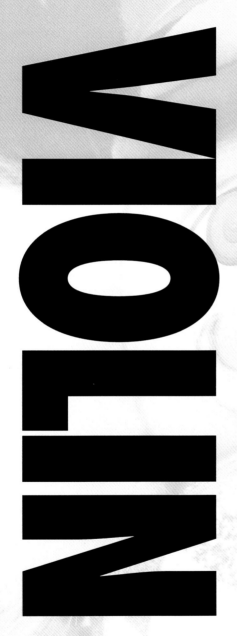

PLAY
Speed · Pitch · Balance

To access audio visit:
www.halleonard.com/mylibrary
Enter Code
2407-3477-4298-7413

Arranged and Recorded by Donald Sosin

HOW TO USE THE AUDIO ACCOMPANIMENT
A melody cue appears on the right channel only. If your stereo or computer has a balance adjustment, you can adjust the volume of the melody by turning down the right channel.

ISBN 978-1-57560-962-1

Copyright © 2007 Cherry Lane Music Company
International Copyright Secured   All Rights Reserved

The music, text, design and graphics in this publication are protected by copyright law. Any duplication or transmission, by any means, electronic, mechanical, photocopying, recording or otherwise, is an infringement of copyright.

Visit Hal Leonard Online at
www.halleonard.com

OVERTURE

By Pyotr Il'yich Tchaikovsky

VIOLIN

This Arrangement Copyright © 2007 Cherry Lane Music Company
International Copyright Secured   All Rights Reserved

3

MARCH

By Pyotr Il'yich Tchaikovsky

VIOLIN

This Arrangement Copyright © 2007 Cherry Lane Music Company
International Copyright Secured   All Rights Reserved

SPANISH DANCE
("Chocolate")

By Pyotr Il'yich Tchaikovsky

VIOLIN

Allegro brillante ♩ = 180

This Arrangement Copyright © 2007 Cherry Lane Music Company
International Copyright Secured   All Rights Reserved

ARABIAN DANCE
("Coffee")

By Pyotr Il'yich Tchaikovsky

VIOLIN

This Arrangement Copyright © 2007 Cherry Lane Music Company
International Copyright Secured   All Rights Reserved

7

CHINESE DANCE
("Tea")

By Pyotr Il'yich Tchaikovsky

VIOLIN

This Arrangement Copyright © 2007 Cherry Lane Music Company
International Copyright Secured   All Rights Reserved

RUSSIAN DANCE
(Trepak)

By Pyotr Il'yich Tchaikovsky

VIOLIN

This Arrangement Copyright © 2007 Cherry Lane Music Company
International Copyright Secured   All Rights Reserved

DANCE OF THE REED FLUTES

By Pyotr Il'yich Tchaikovsky

VIOLIN

This Arrangement Copyright © 2007 Cherry Lane Music Company
International Copyright Secured All Rights Reserved

WALTZ OF THE FLOWERS

By Pyotr Il'yich Tchaikovsky

VIOLIN

This Arrangement Copyright © 2007 Cherry Lane Music Company
International Copyright Secured   All Rights Reserved

DANCE OF THE SUGARPLUM FAIRY

By Pyotr Il'yich Tchaikovsky

VIOLIN

This Arrangement Copyright © 2007 Cherry Lane Music Company
International Copyright Secured   All Rights Reserved

FINAL WALTZ AND APOTHEOSIS

By Pyotr Il'yich Tchaikovsky

VIOLIN

This Arrangement Copyright © 2007 Cherry Lane Music Company
International Copyright Secured   All Rights Reserved

101 SONGS

BIG COLLECTIONS OF FAVORITE SONGS ARRANGED FOR SOLO INSTRUMENTALISTS.

101 BROADWAY SONGS

00154199	Flute	$15.99
00154200	Clarinet	$15.99
00154201	Alto Sax	$15.99
00154202	Tenor Sax	$16.99
00154203	Trumpet	$15.99
00154204	Horn	$15.99
00154205	Trombone	$15.99
00154206	Violin	$15.99
00154207	Viola	$15.99
00154208	Cello	$15.99

101 DISNEY SONGS

00244104	Flute	$17.99
00244106	Clarinet	$17.99
00244107	Alto Sax	$17.99
00244108	Tenor Sax	$17.99
00244109	Trumpet	$17.99
00244112	Horn	$17.99
00244120	Trombone	$17.99
00244121	Violin	$17.99
00244125	Viola	$17.99
00244126	Cello	$17.99

101 MOVIE HITS

00158087	Flute	$15.99
00158088	Clarinet	$15.99
00158089	Alto Sax	$15.99
00158090	Tenor Sax	$15.99
00158091	Trumpet	$15.99
00158092	Horn	$15.99
00158093	Trombone	$15.99
00158094	Violin	$15.99
C0158095	Viola	$15.99
C0158096	Cello	$15.99

101 CHRISTMAS SONGS

00278637	Flute	$15.99
00278638	Clarinet	$15.99
00278639	Alto Sax	$15.99
00278640	Tenor Sax	$15.99
00278641	Trumpet	$15.99
00278642	Horn	$14.99
00278643	Trombone	$15.99
00278644	Violin	$15.99
00278645	Viola	$15.99
00278646	Cello	$15.99

101 HIT SONGS

00194561	Flute	$17.99
00197182	Clarinet	$17.99
00197183	Alto Sax	$17.99
00197184	Tenor Sax	$17.99
00197185	Trumpet	$17.99
00197186	Horn	$17.99
00197187	Trombone	$17.99
00197188	Violin	$17.99
00197189	Viola	$17.99
00197190	Cello	$17.99

101 POPULAR SONGS

00224722	Flute	$17.99
00224723	Clarinet	$17.99
00224724	Alto Sax	$17.99
00224725	Tenor Sax	$17.99
00224726	Trumpet	$17.99
00224727	Horn	$17.99
00224728	Trombone	$17.99
00224729	Violin	$17.99
00224730	Viola	$17.99
00224731	Cello	$17.99

101 CLASSICAL THEMES

00155315	Flute	$15.99
00155317	Clarinet	$15.99
00155318	Alto Sax	$15.99
00155319	Tenor Sax	$15.99
00155320	Trumpet	$15.99
00155321	Horn	$15.99
00155322	Trombone	$15.99
00155323	Violin	$15.99
00155324	Viola	$15.99
00155325	Cello	$15.99

101 JAZZ SONGS

00146363	Flute	$15.99
00146364	Clarinet	$15.99
00146366	Alto Sax	$15.99
00146367	Tenor Sax	$15.99
00146368	Trumpet	$15.99
00146369	Horn	$14.99
00146370	Trombone	$15.99
00146371	Violin	$15.99
00146372	Viola	$15.99
00146373	Cello	$15.99

101 MOST BEAUTIFUL SONGS

00291023	Flute	$16.99
00291041	Clarinet	$16.99
00291042	Alto Sax	$17.99
00291043	Tenor Sax	$17.99
00291044	Trumpet	$16.99
00291045	Horn	$16.99
00291046	Trombone	$16.99
00291047	Violin	$16.99
00291048	Viola	$16.99
00291049	Cello	$17.99

See complete song lists and sample pages at www.halleonard.com

HAL•LEONARD®
www.halleonard.com

Prices, contents and availability subject to change without notice.